1935 ...

read a good book, you needed
either a lot of money or a library card.
Cheap paperbacks were available, but their
poor production generally mirrored the quality
between the covers. One weekend that year,
Allen Lane, Managing Director of The Bodley Head,
having spent the weekend visiting Agatha Christie,
found himself on a platform at Exeter station trying to
find something to read for his journey back to London.
He was appalled by the quality of the material he had to
choose from. Everything that Allen Lane achieved from that
day until his death in 1970 was based on a passionate belief
in the existence of 'a vast reading public for *intelligent*
books at a low price'. The result of his momentous vision
was the birth not only of Penguin, but of the 'paperback
revolution'. Quality writing became available for the price of
a packet of cigarettes, literature became a mass medium
for the first time, a nation of book-borrowers became a
nation of book-buyers – and the very concept of book
publishing was changed for ever. Those founding
principles – of quality and value, with an overarching
belief in the fundamental importance of reading –
have guided everything the company has
done since 1935. Sir Allen Lane's
pioneering spirit is still very much alive
at Penguin in 2005. Here's to
the next 70 years!

MORE THAN A BUSINESS

'We decided it was time to end the almost customary half-hearted manner in which cheap editions were produced – as though the only people who could possibly want cheap editions must belong to a lower order of intelligence. We, however, believed in the existence in this country of a vast reading public for intelligent books at a low price, and staked everything on it'
Sir Allen Lane, 1902–1970

'The Penguin Books are splendid value for sixpence, so splendid that if other publishers had any sense they would combine against them and suppress them'
George Orwell

'More than a business … a national cultural asset'
Guardian

'When you look at the whole Penguin achievement you know that it constitutes, in action, one of the more democratic successes of our recent social history'
Richard Hoggart

The Secret Annexe

(from *The Diary of Anne Frank*)

ANNE FRANK

PENGUIN BOOKS

PENGUIN BOOKS

Published by the Penguin Group
Penguin Books Ltd, 80 Strand, London WC2R ORL, England
Penguin Group (USA) Inc., 375 Hudson Street, New York, New York 10014, USA
Penguin Group (Canada), 10 Alcorn Avenue, Toronto, Ontario, Canada M4V 3B2
(a division of Pearson Penguin Canada Inc.)
Penguin Ireland, 25 St Stephen's Green, Dublin 2, Ireland
(a division of Penguin Books Ltd)
Penguin Group (Australia), 250 Camberwell Road, Camberwell, Victoria 3124,
Australia (a division of Pearson Australia Group Pty Ltd)
Penguin Books India Pvt Ltd, 11 Community Centre,
Panchsheel Park, New Delhi – 110 017, India
Penguin Group (NZ), cnr Airborne and Rosedale Roads, Albany,
Auckland 1310, New Zealand (a division of Pearson New Zealand Ltd)
Penguin Books (South Africa) (Pty) Ltd, 24 Sturdee Avenue,
Rosebank 2196, South Africa

Penguin Books Ltd, Registered Offices: 80 Strand, London WC2R ORL, England

www.penguin.com

The Diary of a Young Girl: The Definitive Edition published, with further previously
unpublished material, in Penguin Books 2001
This extract published as a Pocket Penguin 2005

1

Set in 10.5/12.5pt Monotype Dante
Typeset by Palimpsest Book Production Limited
Polmont, Stirlingshire
Printed in England by Clays Ltd, St Ives plc

Mirjam Pressler, the co-editor, is a prize-winning author and translator.
She lives in Germany.
Susan Massotty, the translator of *The Definitive Edition*, lives in Holland.

Foreword

Anne Frank was born in Frankfurt on 12 June 1929. She died of typhoid and exhaustion in the camp of Bergen-Belsen, three months short of her sixteenth birthday. Her father, Otto H. Frank, was the only member of his immediate family to survive the Holocaust. He died in Basel in 1980.

For her thirteenth birthday Anne Frank received a diary as a present from her father. She kept it from 12 June 1942 to 1 August 1944. In this diary, which she addressed to an imaginary friend called Kitty, Anne wrote about her life – first in Nazi-occupied Amsterdam and then, when the Nazi persecution of Jews forced her family into hiding, in the sealed-off back rooms of an Amsterdam office building. Anne had always dreamed of being a writer and hoped one day to publish her diary.

The last entry is dated 1 August 1944. On 4 August 1944, the eight people hiding in the Secret Annexe were arrested. They had been betrayed. Miep Gies and Bep Voskuijl, the two secretaries working in the building, found Anne's diaries and Miep Gies tucked them away for safekeeping. After the war, when it became clear that Anne, her mother Edith and sister Margot were dead, Miep gave the diaries, unread, to Anne's father, Otto Frank. After long deliberation, Otto Frank decided to fulfil his daughter's wish and publish her diary. He never dreamed that it would be translated into over seventy languages and read by millions worldwide.

This extract from The Definitive Edition of Anne's diary begins on Tuesday, 10 November 1942. Anne had by this point spent over a year in the Annexe, together with her parents and sister and the van Daan family. The two families had just decided to take another person, Albert Dussel, into hiding.

Dearest Kitty,

Great news! We're planning to take an eighth person into hiding with us!

Yes, really. We always thought there was enough room and food for one more person, but we were afraid of placing an even greater burden on Mr Kugler and Mr Kleiman. But since reports of the dreadful things being done to the Jews are getting worse by the day, Father decided to sound out these two gentlemen, and they thought it was an excellent plan. 'It's just as dangerous, whether there are seven or eight,' they noted rightly. Once this was settled, we sat down and mentally went through our circle of acquaintances, trying to come up with a single person who would blend in well with our extended family. This wasn't difficult. After Father had rejected all the van Daan relatives, we chose a dentist named Albert Dussel. He lives with a charming Christian lady who's quite a bit younger than he is. They're probably not married, but that's beside the point. He's known to be quiet and refined, and he seemed, from our superficial acquaintance with him, to be nice. Miep knows him as well, so she'll be able to make the necessary arrangements. If he comes, Mr Dussel will have to sleep in my room instead of Margot, who will have to make do with the folding bed.* We'll ask him to bring along something to fill cavities with.

Yours, Anne

---

* After Dussel arrived, Margot slept in her parents' bedroom.

THURSDAY, 12 NOVEMBER 1942

Dearest Kitty,

Miep came to tell us that she'd been to see Dr Dussel. He asked her the moment she entered the room if she knew of a hiding place and was enormously pleased when Miep said she had something in mind. She added that he'd need to go into hiding as soon as possible, preferably Saturday, but he thought this was highly improbable, since he wanted to bring his records up to date, settle his accounts and attend to a couple of patients. Miep relayed the message to us this morning. We didn't think it was wise to wait so long. All these preparations require explanations to various people who we feel ought to be kept in the dark. Miep went to ask if Dr Dussel couldn't manage to come on Saturday after all, but he said no, and now he's scheduled to arrive on Monday.

I think it's odd that he doesn't jump at our proposal. If they pick him up on the street, it won't help either his records or his patients, so why the delay? If you ask me, it's stupid of Father to humour him.

Otherwise, no news.

Yours, Anne

TUESDAY, 17 NOVEMBER 1942

Dearest Kitty!

Mr Dussel has arrived. Everything went smoothly. Miep told him to be at a certain place in front of the post office at 11.00 a.m., when a man would meet him, and he was at the appointed place at the appointed time. Mr Kleiman went up to him, announced that the man he was expecting to meet was unable to come and asked him to drop by the office to see Miep. Mr Kleiman took a tram back to the office while Mr Dussel followed on foot.

It was eleven-twenty when Mr Dussel tapped on the office door. Miep asked him to remove his coat, so the yellow star couldn't be seen, and brought him to the private office, where Mr Kleiman kept him occupied until the cleaning lady had gone. On the pretext that the private office was needed for something else, Miep took Mr Dussel upstairs, opened the bookcase and stepped inside, while Mr Dussel looked on in amazement.

In the meantime, the seven of us had seated ourselves around the dining-table to await the latest addition to our family with coffee and cognac. Miep first led him into the Frank family's room. He immediately recognized our furniture, but had no idea we were upstairs, just above his head. When Miep told him, he was so astonished he nearly fainted. Thank goodness she didn't leave him in suspense any longer, but brought him upstairs. Mr Dussel sank into a chair and stared at us in dumbstruck silence, as though he thought he could read the truth on our faces. Then he stuttered, 'Aber . . . but are you *nicht* in Belgium? The officer, the auto, they were not coming? Your escape was not working?'

We explained the whole thing to him, about how we'd deliberately spread the rumour of the officer and the car to throw the Germans and anyone else who might come looking for us off the track. Mr Dussel was speechless in the face of such ingenuity, and could do nothing but gaze around in surprise as he explored the rest of our lovely and ultra-practical Annexe. We all had lunch together. Then he had a short nap, joined us for tea, put away the few belongings Miep had been able to bring here in advance and began to feel much more at home.

Especially when we handed him the following typewritten rules and regulations for the Secret Annexe (a van Daan production):

PROSPECTUS AND GUIDE TO THE SECRET ANNEXE

A Unique Facility for the Temporary
Accommodation of Jews and Other
Dispossessed Persons

Open all year round: Located in beautiful, quiet, wooded surroundings in the heart of Amsterdam. No private residences in the vicinity. Can be reached by trams 13 or 17 and also by car and bicycle. For those to whom such transport has been forbidden by the German authorities, it can also be reached on foot. Furnished and unfurnished rooms and apartments are available at all times, with or without meals.

Price: Free.

Diet: Low-fat.

Running water in the bathroom (sorry, no bath) and on various inside and outside walls. Cosy stoves for heating.

Ample storage space for a variety of goods. Two large, modern safes.

Private radio with a direct line to London, New York, Tel Aviv and many other stations. Available to all residents after 6.00 p.m. No listening to forbidden broadcasts, with certain exceptions, i.e. German stations may only be tuned in to listen to classical music. It is absolutely forbidden to listen to German news bulletins (regardless of where they are transmitted from) and to pass them on to others.

Rest hours: From 10.00 p.m. to 7.30 a.m.; 10.15 a.m.

on Sundays. Owing to circumstances, residents are required to observe rest hours during the daytime when instructed to do so by the Management. To ensure the safety of all, rest hours must be strictly observed!!!

Free-time activities: None allowed outside the house until further notice.

Use of language: It is necessary to speak softly at all times. Only the language of civilized people may be spoken, thus no German.

Reading and relaxation: No German books may be read, except for the classics and works of a scholarly nature. Other books are optional.

Callisthenics: Daily.

Singing: Only softly, and after 6.00 p.m.

Films: Prior arrangements required.

Lessons: A weekly correspondence course in shorthand. Courses in English, French, maths and history offered at any hour of the day or night. Payment in the form of tuition, e.g. Dutch.

Separate department for the care of small household pets (with the exception of vermin, for which special permits are required).

Mealtimes:

> *Breakfast:* At 9.00 a.m. daily except public holidays and Sundays; at approximately 11.30 a.m. on Sundays and public holidays.
> *Lunch:* A light meal. From 1.15 p.m. to 1.45 p.m.
> *Dinner:* May or may not be a hot meal. Mealtime depends on news broadcasts.

Obligations with respect to the Supply Corps: Residents must be prepared to help with office work at all times.

Baths: The tin bath is available to all residents after 9.00 a.m. on Sundays. Residents may wash in the downstairs lavatory, kitchen, private office or front office, as they choose.

Alcohol: For medicinal purposes only.

The end.

Yours, Anne

THURSDAY, 19 NOVEMBER 1942

Dearest Kitty,

Just as we thought, Mr Dussel is a very nice man. Of course he didn't mind sharing a room with me; to be honest, I'm not exactly delighted at having a stranger use my things, but you have to make sacrifices for a good cause, and I'm glad I can make this small one. 'If we can save even one of our friends, the rest doesn't matter,' said Father, and he's absolutely right.

The first day Mr Dussel was here, he asked me all sorts of questions – for example, what time the cleaning lady comes to the office, how we've arranged to use the bathroom and when we're allowed to go to the lavatory. You may laugh, but these things aren't so easy in a hiding place. During the daytime we can't make any noise that might be heard downstairs, and when someone else is there, like the cleaning lady, we have to be extra careful. I patiently explained all this to Mr Dussel, but I was surprised to see how slow he is to catch on. He asks everything twice and still can't remember what you've told him.

Maybe he's just confused by the sudden change and he'll get over it. Otherwise, everything is fine.

Mr Dussel has told us much about the outside world

we've missed for so long. He had sad news. Countless friends and acquaintances have been taken off to a dreadful fate. Night after night, green and grey military vehicles cruise the streets. They knock on every door, asking whether any Jews live there. If so, the whole family is immediately taken away. If not, they proceed to the next house. It's impossible to escape their clutches unless you go into hiding. They often go around with lists, knocking only on those doors where they know there's a big haul to be made. They frequently offer a bounty, so much per head. It's like the slave hunts of the olden days. I don't mean to make light of this; it's much too tragic for that. In the evenings when it's dark, I often see long lines of good, innocent people, accompanied by crying children, walking on and on, ordered about by a handful of men who bully and beat them until they nearly drop. No one is spared. The sick, the elderly, children, babies and pregnant women – all are marched to their death.

We're so fortunate here, away from the turmoil. We wouldn't have to give a moment's thought to all this suffering if it weren't for the fact that we're so worried about those we hold dear, whom we can no longer help. I feel wicked sleeping in a warm bed, while somewhere out there my dearest friends are dropping from exhaustion or being knocked to the ground.

I get frightened myself when I think of close friends who are now at the mercy of the cruellest monsters ever to stalk the earth.

And all because they're Jews.

Yours, Anne

Dearest Kitty,

We don't really know how to react. Up till now very little news about the Jews had reached us here, and we thought it best to stay as cheerful as possible. Every now and then Miep used to mention what had happened to a friend, and Mother or Mrs van Daan would start to cry, so she decided it was better not to say any more. But we bombarded Mr Dussel with questions, and the stories he had to tell were so gruesome and dreadful that we can't get them out of our heads. Once we've had time to digest the news, we'll probably go back to our usual joking and teasing. It won't do us or those outside any good if we continue to be as gloomy as we are now. And what would be the point of turning the Secret Annexe into a Melancholy Annexe?

No matter what I'm doing, I can't help thinking about those who are gone. I catch myself laughing and remember that it's a disgrace to be so cheerful. But am I supposed to spend the whole day crying? No, I can't do that. This gloom will pass.

Added to this misery there's another, but of a more personal nature, and it pales in comparison to the suffering I've just told you about. Still, I can't help telling you that lately I've begun to feel deserted. I'm surrounded by too great a void. I never used to give it much thought, since my mind was filled with my friends and having a good time. Now I think either about unhappy things or about myself. It's taken a while, but I've finally realized that Father, no matter how kind he may be, can't take the place of my former world. When it comes to my feelings, Mother and Margot ceased to count long ago.

But why do I bother you with this foolishness? I'm

8

terribly ungrateful, Kitty, I know, but when I've been scolded for the umpteenth time and have all these other woes to think about as well, my head begins to reel!

Yours, Anne

SATURDAY, 28 NOVEMBER 1942

Dearest Kitty,

We've been using too much electricity and have now exceeded our ration. The result: excessive economy and the prospect of having the electricity cut off. No light for a fortnight; that's a pleasant thought, isn't it? But who knows, maybe it won't be so long! It's too dark to read after four or four-thirty, so we while away the time with all kinds of crazy activities: telling riddles, doing callisthenics in the dark, speaking English or French, reviewing books – after a while everything gets boring. Yesterday I discovered a new pastime: using a good pair of binoculars to peek into the lighted rooms of the neighbours. During the day our curtains can't be opened, not even an inch, but there's no harm when it's so dark.

I never knew that neighbours could be so interesting. Ours are, at any rate. I've come across a few at dinner, one family making a cine-film and the dentist opposite working on a frightened old lady.

Mr Dussel, the man who was said to get along so well with children and to absolutely adore them, has turned out to be an old-fashioned disciplinarian and preacher of unbearably long sermons on manners. Since I have the singular pleasure (!) of sharing my far too narrow room with His Excellency, and since I'm generally considered to be the worst behaved of the three young people, it's all I can do to avoid having the same old scoldings and

9

admonitions repeatedly flung at my head and to pretend not to hear. This wouldn't be so bad if Mr Dussel weren't such a telltale and hadn't singled out Mother to be the recipient of his reports. If Mr Dussel's just read me the riot act, Mother lectures me all over again, this time throwing the whole book at me. And if I'm really lucky, Mrs van D. calls me to account five minutes later and lays down the law as well!

Really, it's not easy being the badly brought-up centre of attention of a family of nit-pickers.

In bed at night, as I ponder my many sins and exaggerated shortcomings, I get so confused by the sheer amount of things I have to consider that I either laugh or cry, depending on my mood. Then I fall asleep with the strange feeling of wanting to be different from what I am or being different from what I want to be, or perhaps of behaving differently from what I am or want to be.

Oh dear, now I'm confusing you too. Forgive me, but I don't like crossing things out, and in these times of scarcity, tossing away a piece of paper is clearly taboo. So I can only advise you not to reread the above passage and to make no attempt to get to the bottom of it, because you'll never find your way out again!

Yours, Anne

MONDAY, 7 DECEMBER 1942

Dearest Kitty,

Hanukkah and St Nicholas' Day nearly coincided this year; they were only one day apart. We didn't make much of a fuss with Hanukkah, merely exchanging a few small gifts and lighting the candles. Since candles are in short supply, we lit them for only ten minutes, but as long as we sing the song, that doesn't matter. Mr van Daan made a menorah out of wood, so that was taken care of too.

St Nicholas' Day on Saturday was much more fun. During dinner Bep and Miep were so busy whispering to Father that our curiosity was aroused and we suspected they were up to something. Sure enough, at eight o'clock we all trooped downstairs through the passage in pitch darkness (it gave me the shivers, and I wished I was safely back upstairs!) to the alcove. We could switch on the light, since this room doesn't have any windows. When that was done, Father opened the big cupboard.

'Oh, how wonderful!' we all cried.

In the corner was a large basket decorated with colourful paper and a mask of Black Peter.

We quickly took the basket upstairs with us. Inside was a little gift for everyone, including an appropriate verse. Since you're familiar with the kinds of poems people write each other on St Nicholas' Day, I won't copy them down for you.

I received a doll, Father got bookends, and so on. Well anyway, it was a nice idea, and since the eight of us had never celebrated St Nicholas' Day before, this was a good time to begin.

Yours, Anne

PS. We also had presents for everyone downstairs, a few things left over from the Good Old Days; plus Miep and Bep are always grateful for money.

Today we heard that Mr van Daan's ashtray, Mr Dussel's picture frame and Father's bookends were made by none other than Mr Voskuijl. How anyone can be so clever with his hands is a mystery to me!

Dearest Kitty,

Mr van Daan used to be in the meat, sausage and spice business. He was hired for his knowledge of spices, and yet, to our great delight, it's his sausage talents that have come in handy now.

We ordered a large amount of meat (under the counter, of course) that we were planning to preserve in case there were hard times ahead. Mr van Daan decided to make bratwurst, sausages and mettwurst. I had fun watching him put the meat through the mincer: once, twice, three times. Then he added the remaining ingredients to the minced meat and used a long pipe to force the mixture into the casings. We ate the bratwurst with sauerkraut for lunch, but the sausages, which were going to be preserved, had to dry first, so we hung them over a pole suspended from the ceiling. Everyone who came into the room burst into laughter when they saw the dangling sausages. It was such a comical sight.

The kitchen was a shambles. Mr van Daan, clad in his wife's apron and looking fatter than ever, was working away at the meat. What with his bloody hands, red face and spotted apron, he looked like a real butcher. Mrs van D. was trying to do everything at once: learning Dutch out of a book, stirring the soup, watching the meat, sighing and moaning about her broken rib. That's what happens when old (!) ladies do such stupid exercises to get rid of their fat behinds! Dussel had an eye infection and was sitting next to the stove dabbing his eyes with camomile tea. Pim [Anne's father], seated in the one ray of sunshine coming through the window, kept having to move his chair this way and that to stay out of the way. His rheumatism must have been bothering him because he was slightly hunched

over and was keeping an eye on Mr van Daan with an
agonized expression on his face. He reminded me of those
aged invalids you see in the poorhouse. Peter was romp-
ing around the room with Mouschi, the cat, while Mother,
Margot and I were peeling boiled potatoes. When you get
right down to it, none of us was doing our work properly,
because we were all so busy watching Mr van Daan.

Dussel has opened his dental practice. Just for fun, I'll
describe the session with his very first patient.

Mother was ironing, and Mrs van D., the first victim,
sat down on a chair in the middle of the room. Dussel,
unpacking his case with an air of importance, asked for
some eau-de-Cologne, which could be used as a disinfec-
tant, and Vaseline, which would have to do for wax. He
looked in Mrs van D.'s mouth and found two teeth that
made her wince with pain and utter incoherent cries every
time he touched them. After a lengthy examination
(lengthy as far as Mrs van D. was concerned, since it actually took no longer than two minutes), Dussel began to
scrape out a cavity. But Mrs van D. had no intention of
letting him. She flailed her arms and legs until Dussel
finally let go of his probe and . . . it remained stuck in Mrs
van D.'s tooth. That really did it! Mrs van D. lashed out
wildly in all directions, cried (as much as you can with an
instrument like that in your mouth), tried to remove it,
but only managed to push it in even farther. Mr Dussel
calmly observed the scene, his hands on his hips, while the
rest of the audience roared with laughter. Of course, that
was very mean of us. If it'd been me, I'm sure I would
have yelled even louder. After a great deal of squirming,
kicking, screaming and shouting, Mrs van D. finally
managed to yank the thing out, and Mr Dussel went on

with his work as if nothing had happened. He was so quick that Mrs van D. didn't have time to pull any more shenanigans. But then, he had more help than he's ever had before: no fewer than two assistants; Mr van D. and I performed our job well. The whole scene resembled one of those engravings from the Middle Ages entitled 'A Quack at Work'. In the meantime, however, the patient was getting restless, since she had to keep an eye on 'her' soup and 'her' food. One thing is certain: it'll be a while before Mrs van D. makes another dental appointment!

Yours, Anne

TUESDAY, 22 DECEMBER 1942

Dearest Kitty,

The Annexe was delighted to hear that we'll all be receiving an extra quarter of a pound of butter for Christmas. According to the newspaper, everyone is entitled to half a pound, but they mean those lucky souls who get their ration books from the government, not Jews in hiding like us who can only afford to buy four rather than eight ration books on the black market. Each of us is going to bake something with the butter. This morning I made two cakes and some biscuits. It's very busy upstairs, and Mother has informed me that I'm not to do any studying or reading until all the household tasks have been finished.

Mrs van Daan is lying in bed nursing her bruised rib. She complains all day long, constantly demands that the bandages be changed and is generally dissatisfied with everything. I'll be glad when she gets back on her feet and can clean up after herself because, I must admit, she's extraordinarily hardworking and neat, and as long as she's in good physical and mental condition, she's quite cheerful.

As if I don't hear 'shh, shh' enough during the day because I'm always making 'too much' noise, my dear room-mate has come up with the idea of saying 'shh, shh' to me all night too. According to him, I shouldn't even turn over. I refuse to take any notice of him, and the next time he shushes me, I'm going to shush him right back.

He gets more exasperating and egotistical as the days go by. Except for the first week, I haven't seen even one of the biscuits he so generously promised me. He's particularly infuriating on Sundays, when he switches on the light at the crack of dawn to exercise for ten minutes.

To me, the torment seems to last for hours, since the chairs I use to make my bed longer are constantly being jiggled under my sleepy head. After rounding off his limbering-up exercises with a few vigorous arm swings, His Lordship begins dressing. His underwear is hanging on a hook, so first he lumbers over to get it and then lumbers back, past my bed. But his tie is on the table, so once again he pushes and bumps his way past the chairs.

But I mustn't waste any more of your time griping about disgusting old men. It won't help matters anyway. My plans for revenge, such as unscrewing the light bulb, locking the door and hiding his clothes, have unfortunately had to be abandoned in the interests of peace.

Oh, I'm becoming so sensible! We've got to be reasonable about everything we do here: studying, listening, holding our tongues, helping others, being kind, making compromises and I don't know what else! I'm afraid my common sense, which was in short supply to begin with, will be used up too quickly and I won't have any left by the time the war is over.

Yours, Anne

Dearest Kitty,

This morning I was constantly interrupted, and as a result I haven't been able to finish a single thing I've begun.

We have a new pastime, namely, filling packets with powdered gravy. The gravy is one of Gies & Co.'s products. Mr Kugler hasn't been able to find anyone else to fill the packets, and besides, it's cheaper if we do the job. It's the kind of work they do in prisons. It's incredibly boring and makes us dizzy and giggly.

Terrible things are happening outside. At any time of night and day, poor helpless people are being dragged out of their homes. They're allowed to take only a rucksack and a little cash with them, and even then, they're robbed of these possessions on the way. Families are torn apart; men, women and children are separated. Children come home from school to find that their parents have disappeared. Women return from shopping to find their houses sealed, their families gone. The Christians in Holland are also living in fear because their sons are being sent to Germany. Everyone is scared. Every night hundreds of planes pass over Holland on their way to German cities, to sow their bombs on German soil. Every hour hundreds, or maybe even thousands, of people are being killed in Russia and Africa. No one can keep out of the conflict, the entire world is at war, and even though the Allies are doing better, the end is nowhere in sight.

As for us, we're quite fortunate. Luckier than millions of people. It's quiet and safe here, and we're using our money to buy food. We're so selfish that we talk about 'after the war' and look forward to new clothes and shoes, when actually we should be saving every penny to help others when the war is over, to salvage whatever we can.

The children in this neighbourhood run around in thin shirts and wooden clogs. They have no coats, no socks, no caps and no one to help them. Gnawing on a carrot to still their hunger pangs, they walk from their cold houses through cold streets to an even colder classroom. Things have got so bad in Holland that hordes of children stop passers-by in the streets to beg for a piece of bread.

I could spend hours telling you about the suffering the war has brought, but I'd only make myself more miserable. All we can do is wait, as calmly as possible, for it to end. Jews and Christians alike are waiting, the whole world is waiting, and many are waiting for death.

Yours, Anne

SATURDAY, 30 JANUARY 1943

Dearest Kitty,

I'm seething with rage, yet I can't show it. I'd like to scream, stamp my foot, give Mother a good shaking, cry and I don't know what else because of the nasty words, mocking looks and accusations that she hurls at me day after day, piercing me like arrows from a tightly strung bow, which are nearly impossible to pull from my body. I'd like to scream at Mother, Margot, the van Daans, Dussel and Father too: 'Leave me alone, let me have at least one night when I don't cry myself to sleep with my eyes burning and my head pounding. Let me get away, away from everything, away from this world!' But I can't do that. I can't let them see my doubts, or the wounds they've inflicted on me. I couldn't bear their sympathy or their good-humoured derision. It would only make me want to scream even more.

Everyone thinks I'm showing off when I talk, ridiculous

when I'm silent, insolent when I answer, cunning when I have a good idea, lazy when I'm tired, selfish when I eat one bite more than I should, stupid, cowardly, calculating, etc., etc. All day long I hear nothing but what an exasperating child I am, and although I laugh it off and pretend not to mind, I do mind. I wish I could ask God to give me another personality, one that doesn't antagonize everyone.

But that's impossible. I'm stuck with the character I was born with, and yet I'm sure I'm not a bad person. I do my best to please everyone, more than they'd ever suspect in a million years. When I'm upstairs, I try to laugh it off because I don't want them to see my troubles.

More than once, after a series of absurd reproaches, I've snapped at Mother: 'I don't care what you say. Why don't you just wash your hands of me – I'm a hopeless case.' Of course, she'd tell me not to talk back and virtually ignore me for two days. Then suddenly all would be forgotten and she'd treat me like everyone else.

It's impossible for me to be all smiles one day and venomous the next. I'd rather choose the golden mean, which isn't so golden, and keep my thoughts to myself. Perhaps sometime I'll treat the others with the same contempt as they treat me. Oh, if only I could.

Yours, Anne

FRIDAY, 5 FEBRUARY 1943

Dearest Kitty,

Though it's been ages since I've written to you about the squabbles, there's still no change. In the beginning Mr Dussel took our soon-forgotten clashes very seriously, but now he's grown used to them and no longer tries to mediate.

Margot and Peter aren't exactly what you'd call 'young'; they're both so quiet and boring. Next to them, I stick out like a sore thumb, and I'm always being told, 'Margot and Peter don't act that way. Why don't you follow your sister's example!' I hate that.

I confess that I have absolutely no desire to be like Margot. She's too weak-willed and passive to suit me; she lets herself be swayed by others and always gives way under pressure. I want to have more backbone! But I keep ideas like these to myself. They'd only laugh at me if I offered this in my defence.

During meals the air is filled with tension. Fortunately, the outbursts are sometimes held in check by the 'soup eaters', the people from the office who come up to have a cup of soup for lunch.

This afternoon Mr van Daan again brought up the fact that Margot eats so little. 'I suppose you do it to keep your figure,' he added in a mocking tone.

Mother, who always comes to Margot's defence, said in a loud voice, 'I can't stand that stupid chatter of yours a minute longer.'

Mrs van D. turned red as a beetroot. Mr van D. stared straight ahead and said nothing.

Still, we often have a good laugh. Not long ago Mrs van D. was entertaining us with some bit of nonsense or other. She was talking about the past, about how well she got along with her father and what a flirt he was. 'And you know,' she continued, 'my father told me that if a gentleman ever got fresh, I was to say, "Remember, sir, that I'm a lady," and he'd know what I meant.' We split our sides laughing, as if she'd told us a good joke.

Even Peter, though he's usually quiet, occasionally gives rise to hilarity. He has the misfortune of adoring foreign words without knowing what they mean. One afternoon we couldn't use the lavatory because there were visitors in the office. Unable to wait, he went to the toilet but didn't flush it. To warn us of the unpleasant smell, he tacked a sign to the door: 'RSVP – gas!'. Of course, he meant 'Danger – gas!' but he thought 'RSVP' looked more elegant. He didn't have the faintest idea that it meant 'please reply'.

Yours, Anne

SATURDAY, 27 FEBRUARY 1943

Dearest Kitty,

Pim is expecting the invasion any day now. Churchill has had pneumonia, but is gradually getting better. Gandhi, the champion of Indian freedom, is on one of his umpteenth hunger strikes.

Mrs van D. claims she's fatalistic. But who's the most afraid when the guns go off? None other than Petronella van Daan.

Jan brought along the episcopal letter that the bishops addressed to their parishioners. It was beautiful and inspiring. 'People of the Netherlands, stand up and take action. Each of us must choose our own weapons to fight for the freedom of our country, our people and our religion! Give your help and support. Act now!' This is what they're preaching from the pulpit. Will it do any good? It's definitely too late to help our fellow Jews.

Guess what's happened to us now? The owner of the building sold it without informing Mr Kugler and Mr Kleiman. One morning the new landlord arrived with an architect to look the place over. Thank goodness Mr Kleiman was in the office. He showed the gentlemen all there was to see, with the exception of the Secret Annexe. He claimed he'd left the key at home and the new owner asked no further questions. If only he doesn't come back demanding to see the Annexe. In that case, we'll be in big trouble!

Father emptied a card file for Margot and me and filled it with index cards that are blank on one side. This is to become our reading file, in which Margot and I are supposed to note down the books we've read, the author and the date. I've learned two new words: 'brothel' and 'coquette'. I've bought a separate exercise-book for new words.

There's a new division of butter and margarine. Each person is to get their portion on their own plate. The distribution is very unfair. The van Daans, who always make breakfast for everyone, give themselves one and a half times more than they do us. My parents are much too afraid of an argument to say anything, which is a shame, because I think people like that should always be given a taste of their own medicine.

Yours, Anne

THURSDAY, 4 MARCH 1943

Dearest Kitty,

Mrs van D. has a new nickname – we've started calling her Mrs Beaverbrook. Of course, that doesn't mean anything to you, so let me explain. A certain Mr Beaverbrook often talks on the English radio about what he considers to be the far too lenient bombardment of Germany. Mrs van Daan, who always contradicts everyone, including Churchill and the news reports, is in complete agreement with Mr Beaverbrook. So we thought it would be a good idea for her to be married to him, and since she was flattered by the notion, we've decided to call her Mrs Beaverbrook from now on.

We're getting a new warehouse employee, since the old one is being sent to Germany. That's bad for him but good for us because the new one won't be familiar with the building. We're still afraid of the men who work in the warehouse.

Gandhi is eating again.

The black market is doing a booming business. If we had enough money to pay the ridiculous prices, we could stuff ourselves silly. Our greengrocer buys potatoes from the 'Wehrmacht' and brings them in sacks to the private office. Since he suspects we're hiding here, he makes a point of coming during lunchtime, when the warehouse employees are out.

So much pepper is being ground at the moment that we sneeze and cough with every breath we take. Everyone who comes upstairs greets us with an 'ah-CHOO'. Mrs van D. swears she won't go downstairs; one more whiff of pepper and she's going to be ill.

I don't think Father has a very nice business. Nothing but pectin and pepper. As long as you're in the food business, why not make sweets?

A veritable thunderstorm of words came crashing down on me again this morning. The air flashed with so many coarse expressions that my ears were ringing with 'Anne's bad this' and 'van Daans' good that'. Fire and brimstone!

Yours, Anne

WEDNESDAY, 10 MARCH 1943

Dearest Kitty,

We had a short circuit last night, and besides that, the guns were booming away until dawn. I still haven't got over my fear of planes and shooting, and I crawl into

Father's bed nearly every night for comfort. I know it sounds childish, but wait till it happens to you! The ack-ack guns make so much noise you can't hear your own voice. Mrs Beaverbrook, the fatalist, practically burst into tears and said in a timid little voice, 'Oh, it's so awful. Oh, the guns are so loud!' – which is another way of saying 'I'm so scared'.

It didn't seem nearly as bad by candlelight as it did in the dark. I was shivering, as if I had a temperature, and begged Father to relight the candle. He was adamant: there was to be no light. Suddenly we heard a burst of machine-gun fire, and that's ten times worse than anti-aircraft guns. Mother jumped out of bed and, to Pim's great annoyance, lit the candle. Her resolute answer to his grumbling was, 'After all, Anne is not an ex-soldier!' And that was the end of that!

Have I told you any of Mrs van D.'s other fears? I don't think so. To keep you up to date on the latest adventures in the Secret Annexe, I should tell you this as well. One night Mrs van D. thought she heard loud footsteps in the attic, and she was so afraid of burglars, she woke her husband. At that very same moment, the thieves disappeared, and the only sound Mr van D. could hear was the frightened pounding of his fatalistic wife's heart. 'Oh, Putti!' she cried. (Putti is Mrs van D.'s pet name for her husband.) 'They must have taken all our sausages and dried beans. And what about Peter? Oh, do you think Peter's still safe and sound in his bed?'

'I'm sure they haven't stolen Peter. Stop being such a ninny, and let me get back to sleep!'

Impossible. Mrs van D. was too scared to sleep.

A few nights later the entire van Daan family was awakened by ghostly noises. Peter went to the attic with a torch and – scurry, scurry – what do you think he saw running away? A swarm of enormous rats!

Once we knew who the thieves were, we let Mouschi sleep in the attic and never saw our uninvited guests again . . . at least not at night.

A few evenings ago (it was seven-thirty and still light), Peter went up to the loft to get some old newspapers. He had to hold on tightly to the trapdoor to climb down the ladder. He put down his hand without looking, and nearly fell off the ladder from shock and pain. Without realizing it, he'd put his hand on a large rat, which had bitten him in the arm. By the time he reached us, white as a sheet and with his knees knocking, the blood had soaked through his pyjamas. No wonder he was so shaken – stroking a rat isn't much fun, especially when it takes a chunk out of your arm.

Yours, Anne

THURSDAY, 18 MARCH 1943

My dearest Kitty,

Turkey's entered the war. Great excitement. Anxiously awaiting radio reports.

FRIDAY, 19 MARCH 1943

Dearest Kitty,

In less than an hour, joy was followed by disappointment. Turkey hasn't entered the war yet. It was only a cabinet minister talking about Turkey giving up its neutrality some time soon. The newspaper-seller in Dam Square was shouting 'Turkey on England's side!' and the papers were being snatched out of his hands. This was how we'd heard the encouraging rumour.

Thousand-guilder notes are being declared invalid. That'll be a blow to the black marketeers and others like them, but even more to people in hiding and anyone else with money that can't be accounted for. To turn in a thousand-guilder note, you have to be able to state how you came by it and provide proof. They can still be used to pay taxes, but only until next week. The five-hundred notes will lapse at the same time. Gies & Co. still had some unaccounted-for thousand-guilder notes, which they used to pay their estimated taxes for the coming years, so everything seems to be above board.

Dussel has received an old-fashioned, foot-operated dentist's drill. That means I'll probably be getting a thorough check-up soon.

Dussel is terribly lax when it comes to obeying the rules of the house. Not only does he write letters to his Charlotte, he's also carrying on a chatty correspondence with various other people. Margot, the Annexe's Dutch teacher, has been correcting these letters for him. Father has forbidden him to keep up the practice and Margot has stopped correcting the letters, but I think it won't be long before he starts up again.

The Führer has been talking to wounded soldiers. We heard him on the radio, and it was pathetic. The questions and answers went something like this:

'My name is Heinrich Scheppel.'

'Where were you wounded?'

'Near Stalingrad.'

'What kind of wound is it?'

'Two frostbitten feet and a fracture of the left arm.'

This is an exact report of the hideous puppet show aired on the radio. The wounded seemed proud of their wounds – the more the better. One was so beside himself at the thought of shaking hands (I presume he still had one) with the Führer that he could barely say a word.

I happened to drop Dussel's soap on the floor and step on it. Now there's a whole piece missing. I've already asked Father to compensate him for the damages, especially since Dussel only gets one bar of inferior wartime soap a month.

Yours, Anne

THURSDAY, 25 MARCH 1943

Dearest Kitty,

Mother, Father, Margot and I were sitting quite pleasantly together last night when Peter suddenly came in and whispered in Father's ear. I caught the words 'a barrel falling over in the warehouse' and 'someone fiddling with the door'.

Margot heard it too, but was trying to calm me down, since I'd turned white as chalk and was extremely nervous. The three of us waited while Father and Peter went downstairs. A minute or two later Mrs van Daan came up from where she'd been listening to the radio and told us that Pim had asked her to turn it off and tiptoe upstairs. But you know what happens when you're trying to be quiet – the old stairs creaked twice as loud. Five minutes later Peter and Pim, the colour drained from their faces, appeared again to relate their experiences.

They had positioned themselves under the staircase and waited. Nothing happened. Then all of a sudden they heard a couple of bangs, as if two doors had been slammed shut inside the house. Pim bounded up the stairs, while Peter went to warn Dussel, who finally presented himself upstairs, though not without kicking up a fuss and making a lot of noise. Then we all tiptoed in our stockinged feet to the van Daans on the next floor. Mr van D. had a bad cold and had already gone to bed, so we gathered around his bedside and discussed our suspicions in a whisper. Every time Mr van D. coughed loudly, Mrs van D. and I nearly had a nervous fit. He kept coughing until someone came up with the bright idea of giving him codeine. His cough subsided immediately.

Once again we waited and waited, but heard nothing. Finally we came to the conclusion that the burglars had taken to their heels when they heard footsteps in an otherwise quiet building. The problem now was that the chairs in the private office were neatly grouped around the radio, which was tuned to England. If the burglars had forced the door and the air-raid wardens were to notice it and call the police, there could be very serious repercussions. So Mr van Daan got up, pulled on his coat and trousers, put on his hat and cautiously followed Father down the stairs, with Peter (armed with a heavy hammer, to be on the safe side) right behind him. The ladies (including Margot and me) waited in suspense until the men returned five minutes later and reported that there was no sign of any activity in the building. We agreed not to run any water or flush the toilet; but since everyone's stomach was churning from all the tension, you can imagine the stench after we'd each had a turn in the lavatory.

Incidents like these are always accompanied by other disasters, and this was no exception. Number one: the Westertoren bells stopped chiming, and I'd always found them so comforting. Number two: Mr Voskuijl left early last night, and we weren't sure if he'd given Bep the key and she'd forgotten to lock the door.

But that was of little importance now. The night had just begun, and we still weren't sure what to expect. We were somewhat reassured by the fact that between eight-fifteen

– when the burglar had first entered the building and put our lives in jeopardy – and ten-thirty, we hadn't heard a sound. The more we thought about it, the less likely it seemed that a burglar would have forced a door so early in the evening, when there were still people out on the streets. Besides that, it occurred to us that the warehouse manager at the Keg Company next door might still have been at work. What with the excitement and the thin walls, it's easy to mistake the sounds. Besides, your imagination often plays tricks on you in moments of danger.

So we went to bed, though not to sleep. Father and Mother and Mr Dussel were awake most of the night, and I'm not exaggerating when I say that I hardly got a wink of sleep. This morning the men went downstairs to see if the outside door was still locked, but all was well!

Of course, we gave the entire office staff a blow-by-blow account of the incident, which had been far from pleasant. It's much easier to laugh at these kinds of things after they've happened, and Bep was the only one who took us seriously.

Yours, Anne

PS. This morning the toilet was clogged, and Father had to stick a long wooden pole and fish out several pounds of excrement and strawberry recipes (which is what we use for toilet paper these days). Afterwards we burned the pole.

SATURDAY, 27 MARCH 1943

Dearest Kitty,

We've finished our shorthand course and are now working on improving our speed. Aren't we clever! Let me tell you more about my 'time killers' (this is what I call my courses, because all we ever do is try to make the days go by as quickly as possible so we're that much closer to the end of our time here). I adore mythology, especially the Greek and Roman gods. Everyone here thinks my interest is just a passing fancy, since they've never heard of a teenager with an appreciation of mythology. Well then, I suppose I'm the first!

Mr van Daan has a cold. Or rather, he has a scratchy throat, but he's making an enormous to-do over it. He gargles with camomile tea, coats the roof of his mouth with a tincture of myrrh and rubs Vick on his chest, nose, gums and tongue. And to top it off, he's in a foul mood!

Rauter, some German bigwig, recently gave a speech. 'All Jews must be out of the German-occupied territories before 1 July. The province of Utrecht will be cleansed of Jews [as if they were cockroaches] between 1 April and 1 May, and the provinces of North and South Holland between 1 May and 1 June.' These poor people are being shipped off to filthy slaughterhouses like a herd of sick and neglected cattle. But I'll say no more on the subject. My own thoughts give me nightmares!

One good piece of news is that the Labour Exchange was set on fire in an act of sabotage. A few days later the Register Office also went up in flames. Men posing as German police bound and gagged the guards and managed to destroy some important documents.

Yours, Anne

THURSDAY, 1 APRIL 1943

Dearest Kitty,

I'm not really in the mood for pranks (see the date). On the contrary, today I can safely quote the saying 'Misfortunes never come singly'.

First, Mr Kleiman, our merry ray of sunshine, had another bout of gastro-intestinal haemorrhaging yesterday and will have to stay in bed for at least three weeks. I should tell you that his stomach has been bothering him quite a bit, and there's no cure. Second, Bep has flu. Third, Mr Voskuijl has to go into hospital next week. He probably has an ulcer and will have to undergo surgery. Fourth, the managers of Pomosin Industries came from Frankfurt to discuss the new Opekta deliveries. Father had gone over the important points with Mr Kleiman, and there wasn't enough time to give Mr Kugler a thorough briefing.

The gentlemen arrived from Frankfurt, and Father was already shaking at the thought of how the talks would go. 'If only I could be there, if only I were downstairs,' he exclaimed.

'Go and lie down with your ear to the floor. They'll be brought to the private office, and you'll be able to hear everything.'

Father's face cleared, and yesterday morning at ten-thirty Margot and Pim (two ears are better than one) took up their posts on the floor. By noon the talks weren't finished, but Father was in no shape to continue his listening campaign. He was in agony from having to lie for hours in such an unusual and uncomfortable position. At two-thirty we heard voices in the passage, and I took his place; Margot kept me company. The conversation was so long-winded and boring that I suddenly fell asleep on the cold, hard linoleum. Margot didn't dare touch me for fear they'd hear us, and of course she couldn't shout. I slept for a good half-hour and then awoke with a start, having forgotten every word of the important discussion. Luckily, Margot had paid more attention.

Yours, Anne

Dearest Kitty,

Oh my, another item has been added to my list of sins. Last night I was lying in bed, waiting for Father to tuck me in and say my prayers with me, when Mother came into the room, sat on my bed and asked very gently, 'Anne, Daddy isn't ready. What if I listen to your prayers tonight?'

'No, Mumsie,' I replied.

Mother got up, stood beside my bed for a moment and then slowly walked towards the door. Suddenly she turned, her face contorted with pain, and said, 'I don't want to be angry with you. I can't make you love me!' A few tears slid down her cheeks as she went out of the door.

I lay still, thinking how mean it was of me to reject her so cruelly, but I also knew that I was incapable of answering her any other way. I can't be a hypocrite and pray with her when I don't feel like it. It just doesn't work that way. I felt sorry for Mother – very, very sorry – because for the first time in my life I noticed she wasn't indifferent to my coldness. I saw the sorrow in her face when she talked about not being able to make me love her. It's hard to tell the truth, and yet the truth is that she's the one who's rejected me. She's the one whose tactless comments and cruel jokes about matters I don't think are funny have made me insensitive to any sign of love on her part. Just as my heart sinks every time I hear her harsh words, that's how her heart sank when she realized there was no more love between us.

She cried half the night and didn't get any sleep. Father has avoided looking at me, and if his eyes do happen to meet mine, I can read his unspoken words: 'How can you be so unkind? How dare you make your mother so sad!'

Everyone expects me to apologize, but this is not something I can apologize for, because I told the truth, and sooner or later Mother was bound to find out anyway. I seem to be indifferent to Mother's tears and Father's glances, and I am, because both of them are now feeling what I've always felt. I can only feel sorry for Mother, who will have to decide what her attitude should be all by herself. For my part, I will continue to remain silent and aloof, and I don't intend to shrink from the truth, because the longer it's postponed, the harder it will be for them to accept it when they do hear it!

Yours, Anne

TUESDAY, 27 APRIL 1943

Dearest Kitty,

The house is still trembling from the after-effects of the quarrels. Everyone is angry with everyone else: Mother and I, Mr van Daan and Father, Mother and Mrs van D. Terrific atmosphere, don't you think? Once again Anne's usual list of shortcomings has been extensively aired.

Our German visitors were back last Saturday. They stayed until six. We all sat upstairs, not daring to move an inch. If there's no one else working in the building or in the neighbourhood, you can hear every single step in the private office. I've got ants in my pants again from having to sit still so long.

Mr Voskuijl has been hospitalized, but Mr Kleiman's back at the office. His stomach stopped bleeding sooner than it normally does. He told us that the Register Office took an extra beating because the firemen flooded the entire building instead of just putting out the fire. That does my heart good!

The Carlton Hotel has been destroyed. Two British planes loaded with firebombs landed right on top of the German Officers' Club. The entire corner of Vijzelstraat and Singel has gone up in flames. The number of air strikes on German cities is increasing daily. We haven't had a good night's rest in ages, and I have bags under my eyes from lack of sleep.

Our food is terrible. Breakfast consists of plain, unbuttered bread and ersatz coffee. For the last two weeks lunch has been either spinach or cooked lettuce with huge potatoes that have a rotten, sweetish taste. If you're trying to slim, the Annexe is the place to be! Upstairs they complain bitterly, but we don't think it's such a tragedy.

All the Dutch men who either fought or were mobilized in 1940 have been called up to work in prisoner-of-war camps. I bet they're taking this precaution because of the invasion!

Yours, Anne

SATURDAY, 1 MAY 1943

Dearest Kitty,

Yesterday was Dussel's birthday. At first he acted as if he didn't want to celebrate it, but when Miep arrived with a large shopping bag overflowing with gifts, he was as excited as a little child. His darling 'Lotje' has sent him eggs, butter, biscuits, lemonade, bread, cognac, spice cake, flowers, oranges, chocolate, books and writing paper. He piled his presents on a table and displayed them for no fewer than three days, the ridiculous old fool!

You mustn't get the idea that he's starving. We found bread, cheese, jam and eggs in his cupboard. It's absolutely disgraceful that Dussel, whom we've treated with such

33

kindness and whom we took in to save from destruction, should stuff himself behind our backs and not give us anything. After all, we've shared all we had with him! But what's worse, in our opinion, is that he's so stingy with respect to Mr Kleiman, Mr Voskuijl and Bep. He doesn't give them a thing. In Dussel's view the oranges that Kleiman so badly needs for his sick stomach will benefit his own stomach even more.

Tonight the guns have been banging away so much that I've already had to gather up my belongings four times. Today I packed a suitcase with the stuff I'd need in case we had to flee, but as Mother correctly noted, 'Where would you go?'

All of Holland is being punished for the workers' strikes. Martial law has been declared, and everyone is going to get one less butter coupon. What naughty children.

I washed Mother's hair this evening, which is no easy task these days. We have to use a very sticky liquid cleanser because there's no more shampoo. Besides that, Mums had a hard time combing her hair because the family comb has only ten teeth left.

Yours, Anne

SUNDAY, 2 MAY 1943

When I think about our lives here, I usually come to the conclusion that we live in a paradise compared with the Jews who aren't in hiding. All the same, later on, when everything has returned to normal, I'll probably wonder how we, who always lived in such comfortable circumstances, could have 'sunk' so low. With respect to manners, I mean. For example, the same oilcloth has covered the dining-table ever since we've been here. After so much use, it's hardly what you'd call spotless. I do my best to clean it, but since the dishcloth was also purchased before we went into hiding and consists of more holes than cloth, it's a thankless task. The van Daans have been sleeping all winter long on the same flannelette sheet, which can't be washed because soap powder is rationed and in short supply. Besides, it's of such poor quality that it's practically useless. Father is walking around in frayed trousers, and his tie is also showing signs of wear and tear. Mummy's corset snapped today and is beyond repair, while Margot is wearing a bra that's two sizes too small. Mother and Margot have shared the same three vests the entire winter, and mine are so small they don't even cover my stomach. These are all things that can be overcome, but I sometimes wonder: how can we, whose every possession, from my knickers to Father's shaving brush, is so old and worn, ever hope to regain the position we had before the war?

SUNDAY, 2 MAY 1943

The Attitude of the Annexe Residents Towards the War

Mr van Daan. In the opinion of us all, this revered gentleman has great insight into politics. Nevertheless, he predicts we'll have to stay here until the end of '43. That's a very long time, and yet it's possible to hold out until then. But who can assure us that this war, which has caused nothing but pain and sorrow, will then be over? And that nothing will have happened to us and our helpers long before that time? No one! That's why each and every day is filled with tension. Expectation and hope generate tension, as does fear – for example, when we hear a noise inside or outside the house, when the guns go off or when we read new 'proclamations' in the paper, since we're afraid our helpers might be forced to go into hiding themselves sometime. These days everyone is talking about having to hide. We don't know how many people are actually in hiding; of course, the number is relatively small compared with the general population, but later on we'll no doubt be astonished at how many good people in Holland were willing to take Jews and Christians, with or without money, into their homes. There's also an unbelievable number of people with false identity papers.

Mrs van Daan. When this beautiful damsel (by her own account) heard that it was getting easier these days to obtain false IDs, she immediately proposed that we each have one made. As if there were nothing to it, as if Father and Mr van Daan were made of money.

Mrs van Daan is always saying the most ridiculous things, and her Putti is often exasperated. But that's not surprising, because one day Kerli announces, 'When this is all over, I'm going to have myself baptized'; and the next, 'As long as I can remember, I've wanted to go to Jerusalem. I only feel at home with other Jews!'

Pim is a big optimist, but he always has his reasons.

Mr Dussel makes up everything as he goes along, and anyone wishing to contradict His Majesty had better think twice. In Albert Dussel's home his word is law, but that doesn't suit Anne Frank in the least.

What the other members of the Annexe family think about the war doesn't matter. When it comes to politics, these four are the only ones who count. Actually, only two of them do, but Madame van Daan and Dussel include themselves as well.

Dearest Kit,

I recently witnessed a fierce dogfight between German and English pilots. Unfortunately, a couple of Allied airmen had to jump out of their burning plane. Our milkman, who lives in Halfweg, saw four Canadians sitting along the side of the road, and one of them spoke fluent Dutch. He asked the milkman if he had a light for his cigarette, and then told him the crew had consisted of six men. The pilot had been burned to death, and the fifth crew member had hidden himself somewhere. The German Security Police came to pick up the four remaining men, none of whom was injured. After parachuting out of a flaming plane, how can anyone have such presence of mind?

Although it's undeniably hot, we have to light a fire every other day to burn our vegetable peelings and rubbish. We can't throw anything into the dustbins, because the warehouse employees might see it. One small act of carelessness and we're done for!

All university students are being asked to sign an official statement to the effect that they 'sympathize with the Germans and approve of the New Order'. Eighty per cent have decided to obey the dictates of their conscience, but the penalty will be severe. Any student refusing to sign will be sent to a German labour camp. What's to become of the youth of our country if they've all got to do hard labour in Germany?

Last night the guns were making so much noise that Mother shut the window; I was in Pim's bed. Suddenly, right above our heads, we heard Mrs van D. leap up, as if she'd been bitten by Mouschi. This was followed by a loud boom, which sounded as if a firebomb had landed beside my bed. 'Lights! Lights!' I screamed.

Pim switched on the lamp. I expected the room to burst into flames any minute. Nothing happened. We all rushed upstairs to see what was going on. Mr and Mrs van D. had seen a red glow through the open window, and he thought there was a fire nearby, while she was certain our house was ablaze. Mrs van D. was already standing beside her bed with her knees knocking when the boom came. Dussel stayed upstairs to smoke a cigarette, and we crawled back into bed. Less than fifteen minutes later the shooting started again. Mrs van D. sprang out of bed and went downstairs to Dussel's room to seek the comfort she was unable to find with her spouse. Dussel welcomed her with the words 'Come into my bed, my child!'

We burst into peals of laughter, and the roar of the guns bothered us no more; our fears had all been swept away.

Yours, Anne

SUNDAY, 13 JUNE 1943

Dearest Kitty,

The poem Father composed for my birthday is too nice to keep to myself.

Since Pim writes his verses only in German, Margot volunteered to translate it into Dutch. See for yourself whether Margot hasn't done herself proud. It begins with the usual summary of the year's events and then continues:

> *As youngest among us, but small no more,*
> *Your life can be trying, for we have the chore*

Of becoming your teachers, a terrible bore.
'We've got experience! Take it from me!'
'We've done this all before, you see.
We know the ropes, we know the game.'
Since time immemorial, always the same.
One's own shortcomings are nothing but fluff,
But everyone else's are heavier stuff.
Fault-finding comes easy when this is our plight,
But it's hard for your parents, try as they might,
To treat you with fairness, and kindness as well;
Nit-picking's a habit that's hard to dispel.
When you're living with old folk, all you can do
Is put up with their nagging – it's hard but it's true.
The pill may be bitter, but down it must go,
For it's meant to keep the peace, you know.
The many months here have not been in vain,
Since wasting time goes against your grain.
You read and study nearly all the day,
Determined to chase the boredom away.
The more difficult question, much harder to bear,
Is 'What on earth do I have to wear?
I've got no more knickers, my clothes are too tight,
My vest is a loincloth, I'm really a sight!
To put on my shoes I must cut off my toes,
Oh dear, I'm plagued with so many woes!'

Margot had trouble getting the part about food to rhyme, so I'm leaving it out. But aside from that, don't you think it's a good poem?

For the rest, I've been thoroughly spoiled and have received a number of lovely presents, including a big book on my favourite subject, Greek and Roman mythology. Nor can I complain about the lack of sweets; everyone had dipped into their last reserves. As the Benjamin of the Annexe, I got more than I deserve.

Yours, Anne

TUESDAY, 15 JUNE 1943

Dearest Kitty,

Heaps of things have happened, but I often think I'm boring you with my dreary chitchat and that you'd just as soon have fewer letters. So I'll keep the news brief.

Mr Voskuijl wasn't operated on for his ulcer after all. Once the doctors had him on the operating table and opened him up, they saw that he had cancer. It was in such an advanced stage that an operation was pointless. So they stitched him up again, kept him in hospital for three weeks, fed him well and sent him back home. But they made an unforgivable error: they told the poor man exactly what was in store for him. He can't work any more, and he's just sitting at home, surrounded by his eight children, brooding about his approaching death. I feel very sorry for him and hate not being able to go out; otherwise, I'd visit him as often as I could and help take his mind off matters. Now the good man can no longer let us know what's being said and done in the warehouse, which is a disaster for us. Mr Voskuijl was our greatest source of help and support when it came to safety measures. We miss him very much.

Next month it's our turn to hand over our radio to the authorities. Mr Kleiman has a small set hidden in his home that he's giving us to replace our beautiful Philips. It's a pity we have to turn in our big one, but when you're in hiding, you can't afford to bring the authorities down on your heads. Of course, we'll put the 'baby' radio upstairs.

What's a clandestine radio when there are already clandestine Jews and clandestine money?

All over the country people are trying to get hold of an old radio that they can hand over instead of their 'morale booster'. It's true: as the reports from outside grow worse and worse, the radio, with its wondrous voice, helps us not to lose heart and to keep telling ourselves, 'Cheer up, keep your spirits high, things are bound to get better!'

Yours, Anne

SUNDAY, II JULY 1943

Dear Kitty,

To get back to the subject of child-rearing (for the umpteenth time), let me tell you that I'm doing my best to be helpful, friendly and kind and to do all I can to keep the rain of rebukes down to a light drizzle. It's not easy trying to behave like a model child with people you can't stand, especially when you don't mean a word of it. But I can see that a little hypocrisy gets me a lot further than my old method of saying exactly what I think (even though no one ever asks my opinion or cares one way or another). Of course, I often forget my role and find it impossible to curb my anger when they're unfair, so that they spend the next month saying I'm the cheekiest girl in the world. Don't you think I'm to be pitied sometimes? It's a good thing I'm not a moaner, because then I might become sour and bad-tempered. I can usually see the humorous side of their scoldings, but it's easier when somebody else is being hauled over the coals.

Further, I've decided (after a great deal of thought) to drop the shorthand. First, so that I have more time for my other subjects, and second, because of my eyes. That's a sad story. I've become very short-sighted and should have had glasses ages ago. (Ugh, won't I look like a muggins!) But as you know, people in hiding can't . . .

Yesterday all anyone here could talk about was Anne's eyes, because Mother had suggested I go to the specialist with Mrs Kleiman. Just hearing this made my knees weak, since it's no small matter. Going outside! Just think of it, walking down the *street*! I can't imagine it. I was petrified at first, and then glad. But it's not as simple as all that; the various authorities who had to approve such a step were unable to reach a quick decision. They first had to carefully weigh all the difficulties and risks, though Miep was ready to set off immediately with me in tow. In the meantime, I'd taken my grey coat from the wardrobe, but it was so small it looked as if it might have belonged to my little sister. We lowered the hem, but I still couldn't button it. I'm really curious to see what they decide, only I don't think they'll ever work out a plan, because the British have landed in Sicily and Father's all set for a 'quick finish'.

Bep's been giving Margot and me a lot of office work to do. It makes us both feel important, and it's a big help to her. Anyone can file letters and make entries in a sales book, but we do it with remarkable accuracy.

Miep has so much to carry she looks like a pack mule. She goes out nearly every day in search of vegetables, and then cycles back with her purchases in large shopping bags. She's also the one who brings five library books with her every Saturday. We long for Saturdays because that means books. We're like a lot of little children with a present. Ordinary people don't know how much books can mean to someone who's cooped up. Our only diversions are reading, studying and listening to the wireless.

Yours, Anne

The Best Little Table

Yesterday afternoon Father gave me permission to ask Mr Dussel whether he would please be so good as to allow me (see how polite I am?) to use the table in our room two afternoons a week, from four to five-thirty. I already sit there every day from two-thirty to four while Dussel has a nap, but the rest of the time the room and the table are out of bounds to me. It's impossible to study next door in the afternoon, because there's too much going on. Besides, Father sometimes likes to sit at the desk during the afternoon.

So it seemed like a reasonable request, and I asked Dussel very politely. What do you think the learned gentleman's reply was? 'No.' Just plain 'No'!

I was incensed and wasn't about to let myself be put off like that. I asked him the reason for his 'No', but this didn't get me anywhere. The gist of his reply was: 'I have to study too, you know, and if I can't do that in the afternoons, I won't be able to fit it in at all. I have to finish the task I've set for myself; otherwise, there's no point in starting. Besides, you aren't serious about your studies. Mythology – what kind of work is that? Reading and knitting don't count either. I use that table and I'm not going to give it up!'

I replied, 'Mr Dussel, I do take my work seriously. I can't study next door in the afternoons, and I would appreciate it if you would reconsider my request!'

Having said these words, the insulted Anne turned round and pretended the learned doctor wasn't there. I was seething with rage and felt that Dussel had been incredibly rude (which he certainly had been) and that I'd been very polite.

That evening, when I managed to get hold of Pim, I told him what had happened and we discussed what my next step should be, because I had no intention of giving up and preferred to deal with the matter myself. Pim gave me a rough idea of how to approach Dussel, but cautioned me to wait until the next day, since I was in such a flap. I ignored this last piece of advice and waited for Dussel after I'd done the washing-up. Pim was sitting next door and that had a calming effect.

I began, 'Mr Dussel, you seem to believe further discussion of the matter is pointless, but I beg you to reconsider.'

Dussel gave me his most charming smile and said, 'I'm always prepared to discuss the matter, even though it's already been settled.'

I went on talking, despite Dussel's repeated interruptions. 'When you first came here,' I said, 'we agreed that the room was to be shared by the two of us. If we were to divide it fairly, you'd have the entire morning and I'd have the entire afternoon! I'm not asking for that much, but two afternoons a week does seem reasonable to me.'

Dussel leapt out of his chair as if he'd sat on a pin. 'You have no business talking about your rights to the room. Where am I supposed to go? Maybe I should ask Mr van Daan to build me a cubbyhole in the attic. You're not the only one who can't find a quiet place to work. You're always looking for a fight. If your sister Margot, who has more right to work space than you do, had come to me with the same request, I'd never even have thought of refusing, but you . . .'

And once again he brought up the business about the mythology and the knitting, and once again Anne was insulted. However, I showed no sign of it and let Dussel finish: 'But no, it's impossible to talk to you. You're shamefully self-centred. No one else matters, as long as you get your way. I've never seen such a child. But after all is said and done, I'll be obliged to let you have your way, since I don't want people saying later on that Anne Frank failed her exams because Mr Dussel refused to relinquish his table!'

He went on and on until there was such a deluge of words I could hardly keep up. For one fleeting moment I thought, 'Him and his lies. I'll smack his ugly mug so hard he'll go bouncing off the wall!' But the next moment I thought, 'Calm down, he's not worth getting so upset about!'

At long last Mr Dussel's fury was spent, and he left the room with an expression of triumph mixed with wrath, his coat pockets bulging with food.

I went running over to Father and recounted the entire story, or at least those parts he hadn't been able to follow himself. Pim decided to talk to Dussel that very same evening, and they spoke for more than half an hour. They first discussed whether Anne should be allowed to use the table, yes or no. Father said that he and Dussel had dealt with the subject once before, at which time he'd professed to agree with Dussel because he didn't want to contradict the elder in front of the younger, but that, even then, he hadn't thought it was fair. Dussel felt I had no right to talk as if he were an intruder laying claim to everything in sight. But Father protested strongly, since he himself had heard me say nothing of the kind. And so the conversation went back and forth, with Father defending my 'selfishness' and my 'pointless activities' and Dussel grumbling the whole time.

Dussel finally had to give in, and I was granted the opportunity to work without interruption two afternoons a week. Dussel looked very sullen, didn't speak to me for two days and made sure he occupied the table from five to five-thirty – all very childish, of course.

Anyone who's so petty and pedantic at the age of fifty-four was born that way and is never going to change.

Dearest Kitty,

There's been another break-in, but this time a real one! Peter went down to the warehouse this morning at seven, as usual, and noticed at once that both the warehouse door and the street door were open. He immediately reported this to Pim, who went to the private office, tuned the radio to a German station and locked the door. Then they both went back upstairs. In such cases our orders are 'not to wash ourselves or run any water, to be quiet, to be dressed by eight and not to go to the lavatory', and as usual we followed these to the letter. We were all glad we'd slept so well and hadn't heard anything. For a while we were indignant because no one from the office came upstairs the entire morning; Mr Kleiman left us on tenterhooks until eleven-thirty. He told us that the burglars had forced the outside door and the warehouse door with a crowbar, but when they didn't find anything worth stealing, they tried their luck on the next floor. They stole two cash-boxes containing 40 guilders, blank chequebooks and, worst of all, coupons for 330 pounds of sugar, our entire allotment. It won't be easy to wangle new ones.

Mr Kugler thinks this burglar belongs to the same gang as the one who made an unsuccessful attempt six weeks ago to open all three doors (the warehouse door and the two outside doors).

The burglary caused another stir, but the Annexe seems

to thrive on excitement. Naturally, we were glad the cash register and the typewriters had been safely tucked away in our wardrobe.

Yours, Anne

PS. Landing in Sicily. Another step closer to the . . . !

MONDAY, 19 JULY 1943

Dearest Kitty,

North Amsterdam was very heavily bombed on Sunday. There was apparently a great deal of destruction. Entire streets are in ruins, and it will take a while for them to dig out all the bodies. So far there have been two hundred dead and countless wounded; the hospitals are bursting at the seams. We've been told of children searching forlornly in the smouldering ruins for their dead parents. It still makes me shiver to think of the dull, distant drone that signified the approaching destruction.

FRIDAY, 23 JULY 1943

Bep is currently able to get hold of exercise-books, especially journals and ledgers, useful for my bookkeeping sister! Other kinds are for sale as well, but don't ask what they're like or how long they'll last. At the moment they're all labelled 'No Coupons Needed'! Like everything else you can purchase without ration stamps, they're totally worthless. They consist of twelve sheets of grey paper with narrow lines that slant across the page. Margot is thinking about taking a course in calligraphy; I've advised her to go ahead and do it. Mother won't let me because of my eyes, but I think that's silly. Whether I do that or something else, it all comes down to the same thing.

Since you've never been through a war, Kitty, and since you know very little about life in hiding, in spite of my letters, let me tell you, just for fun, what we each want to do first when we're able to go outside again.

Margot and Mr van Daan wish, above all else, to have a hot bath, filled to the brim, which they can lie in for more than half an hour. Mrs van Daan would like a cake, Dussel can think of nothing but seeing his Charlotte, and Mother is dying for a cup of real coffee. Father would like to visit Mr Voskuijl, Peter would go into town, and as for me, I'd be so overjoyed I wouldn't know where to begin.

Most of all I long to have a home of our own, to be able to move around freely and have someone help me with my homework again, at last. In other words, to go back to school!

Bep has offered to get us some fruit, at so-called bargain prices: grapes 2.50 guilders a pound, gooseberries 70 cents a pound, one peach 50 cents, melons 75 cents a pound. No wonder the papers write every evening in big, fat letters: 'Play Fair and Keep Prices Down'!

MONDAY, 26 JULY 1943

Dear Kitty,

Yesterday was a very tumultuous day, and we're still all wound up. Actually, you may wonder if there's ever a day that passes without some kind of excitement.

The first warning siren went off in the morning while we were at breakfast, but we paid no attention, because it only meant that the planes were crossing the coast. I had a terrible headache, so I lay down for an hour after breakfast and then went to the office at about two. At two-thirty Margot had finished her office work and was just gathering her things together when the sirens began wailing again. So she and I trooped back upstairs. None too soon, it seems, for less than five minutes later the guns were booming so loudly that we went and stood in the passage. The house shook and the bombs kept falling. I was clutching my 'escape bag', more because I wanted to have something to hold on to than because I wanted to run away. I know we can't leave here, but if we had to, being seen on the streets would be just as dangerous as getting caught in an air raid. After half an hour the drone of engines faded and the house began to hum with activity again. Peter emerged from his lookout post in the front attic, Dussel remained in the front office, Mrs van D. felt safest in the private office, Mr van Daan had been watching from the loft, and those of us on the landing spread out to watch the columns of smoke rising from the harbour. Before long the smell of fire was everywhere, and outside it looked as if the city were enveloped in a thick fog.

A big fire like that is not a pleasant sight, but fortunately for us it was all over, and we went back to our various jobs. Just as we were starting dinner: another air-raid alarm. The food was good, but I lost my appetite the moment I heard the siren. Nothing happened, however, and forty-five minutes later the all-clear was sounded. After the washing-up: another air-raid warning, gunfire and swarms of planes. 'Oh, gosh, twice in one day,' we thought, 'that's twice too many.' Little good that did us, because once again the bombs rained down, this time on the other side of the city. According to British reports, Schiphol Airport was bombed. The planes dived and climbed, the air was abuzz with the drone of engines. It was very scary, and the whole time I kept thinking, 'Here it comes, this is it.'

I can assure you that when I went to bed at nine, my legs were still shaking. At the stroke of midnight I woke up again: more planes! Dussel was undressing, but I took no notice and leapt up, wide awake, at the sound of the first shot. I stayed in Father's bed until one, in my own bed until one-thirty, and was back in Father's bed at two. But the planes kept on coming. At last they stopped firing and I was able to go back 'home' again. I finally fell asleep at half past two.

Seven o'clock. I awoke with a start and sat up in bed. Mr van Daan was with Father. My first thought was: burglars. 'Everything,' I heard Mr van Daan say, and I thought everything had been stolen. But no, this time it was wonderful news, the best we've had in months, maybe even since the war began. Mussolini has resigned and the King of Italy has taken over the government.

We jumped for joy. After the awful events of yesterday, finally something good happens and brings us . . . hope! Hope for an end to the war, hope for peace.

Mr Kugler popped in and told us that the Fokker aircraft factory had been hit hard. Meanwhile, there was another air-raid alarm this morning, with planes flying over, and another warning siren. I've had it up to here with alarms. I've hardly slept, and the last thing I want to do is work. But now the suspense about Italy and the hope that the war will be over by the end of the year are keeping us awake . . .

Yours, Anne

THURSDAY, 29 JULY 1943

Dearest Kitty,

Mrs van Daan, Dussel and I were doing the washing-up, and I was extremely quiet. This is very unusual for me and they were sure to notice, so in order to avoid any questions, I quickly racked my brains for a neutral topic. I thought the book *Henry from Across the Street* might fit the bill, but I couldn't have been more wrong; if Mrs van Daan doesn't jump down my throat, Mr Dussel does. It all boiled down to this: Mr Dussel had recommended the book to Margot and me as an example of excellent writing. We thought it was anything but that. The little boy had been portrayed well, but as for the rest . . . the less said the better. I mentioned something to that effect while we were washing up, and Dussel launched into a veritable tirade.

'How can you possibly understand the psychology of a man? That of a child isn't so difficult [!]. But you're far too young to read a book like that. Even a twenty-year-old man would be unable to comprehend it.' (So why did he go out of his way to recommend it to Margot and me?)

Mrs van D. and Dussel continued their harangue: 'You know far too much about things you're not supposed to. You've been brought up all wrong. Later on, when you're older, you won't be able to enjoy anything any more. You'll say, "Oh, I read that twenty years ago in some book." You'd better hurry if you want to catch a husband or fall in love, since everything is bound to be a disappointment to you. You already know all there is to know in theory. But in practice? That's another story!'

Can you imagine how I felt? I astonished myself by calmly replying, 'You may think I haven't been raised properly, but many people would disagree!'

They apparently believe that good child-rearing includes trying to pit me against my parents, since that's all they ever do. And not telling a girl my age about grown-up subjects is fine. We can all see what happens when people are raised that way.

At that moment I could have slapped them both for

poking fun at me. I was beside myself with rage, and if I only knew how much longer we had to put up with each other's company, I'd start counting the days.

Mrs van Daan's a fine one to talk! She sets an example all right – a bad one! She's known to be exceedingly pushy, egotistical, cunning, calculating and perpetually dissatisfied. Add to that, vanity and coquettishness and there's no question about it: she's a thoroughly despicable person. I could write an entire book about Madame van Daan, and who knows, maybe someday I will. Anyone can put on a charming exterior when they want to. Mrs van D. is friendly to strangers, especially men, so it's easy to make a mistake when you first get to know her.

Mother thinks that Mrs van D. is too stupid for words, Margot that she's too unimportant, Pim that she's too ugly (literally and figuratively!), and after long observation (I'm never prejudiced at the beginning), I've come to the conclusion that she's all three of the above, and lots more besides. She has so many bad traits, why should I single out just one of them?

Yours, Anne

PS. Will the reader please take into consideration that this story was written before the writer's fury had cooled?

TUESDAY, 3 AUGUST 1943

Dearest Kitty,

Things are going well on the political front. Italy has banned the Fascist Party. The people are fighting the Fascists in many places – even the army has joined the fight. How can a country like that continue to wage war against England?

Our beautiful radio was taken away last week. Dussel

was very angry at Mr Kugler for turning it in on the appointed day. Dussel is slipping lower and lower in my estimation, and he's already below zero. Whatever he says about politics, history, geography or anything else is so ridiculous that I hardly dare repeat it: Hitler will fade from history; the harbour in Rotterdam is bigger than the one in Hamburg; the English are idiots for not taking the opportunity to bomb Italy to smithereens; etc., etc.

We just had a third air raid. I decided to grit my teeth and practise being courageous.

Mrs van Daan, the one who always said 'Let them fall' and 'Better to end with a bang than not to end at all', is the most cowardly one among us. She was shaking like a leaf this morning and even burst into tears. She was comforted by her husband, with whom she recently declared a truce after a week of squabbling; I nearly got sentimental at the sight.

Mouschi has now proved, beyond a shadow of a doubt, that having a cat has disadvantages as well as advantages. The whole house is crawling with fleas, and it's getting worse each day. Mr Kleiman sprinkled yellow powder in every nook and cranny, but the fleas haven't taken the slightest notice. It's making us all very jittery; we're forever imagining a bite on our arms and legs or other parts of our bodies, so we leap up and do a few exercises, since it gives us an excuse to take a better look at our arms or necks. But now we're paying the price for having had so little physical exercise; we're so stiff we can hardly turn our heads. The real callisthenics fell by the wayside long ago.

Yours, Anne

Dearest Kitty,

Now that we've been in hiding for a little over a year, you know a great deal about our lives. Still, I can't possibly tell you everything, since it's all so different compared with ordinary times and ordinary people. Nevertheless, to give you a closer look into our lives, from time to time I'll describe part of an ordinary day. I'll start with the evening and night.

Nine in the evening. Bedtime always begins in the Annexe with an enormous hustle and bustle. Chairs are shifted, beds pulled out, blankets unfolded – nothing stays where it is during the daytime. I sleep on a small divan, which is only five feet long, so we have to add a few chairs to make it longer. Eiderdown, sheets, pillows, blankets: everything has to be removed from Dussel's bed, where it's kept during the day.

In the next room there's a terrible creaking: that's Margot's folding bed being set up. More blankets and pillows, anything to make the wooden slats a bit more comfortable. Upstairs it sounds like thunder, but it's only Mrs van D.'s bed being shoved against the window so that Her Majesty, arrayed in her pink bed jacket, can sniff the night air through her delicate little nostrils.

Nine o'clock. After Peter's finished, it's my turn for the bathroom. I wash myself from head to toe, and more often than not I find a tiny flea floating in the sink (only during the hot months, weeks or days). I brush my teeth, curl my hair, manicure my nails and dab peroxide on my upper lip to bleach the black hairs – all this in less than half an hour.

Nine-thirty. I throw on my dressing-gown. With soap in one hand, and potty, hairpins, knickers, curlers and cotton wool in the other, I hurry out of the bathroom. The next person in invariably calls me back to remove the grace-fully curved but unsightly hairs that I've left in the sink.

Ten o'clock. Time to put up the black-out screen and say good night. For the next fifteen minutes, at least, the house is filled with the creaking of beds and the sigh of broken springs, and then, provided our upstairs neighbours aren't having a marital tiff in bed, all is quiet.

Eleven-thirty. The bathroom door creaks. A narrow strip of light falls into the room. Squeaking shoes, a large coat, even larger than the man inside it . . . Dussel is returning from his nightly work in Mr Kugler's office. I hear him shuffling back and forth for ten whole minutes, the rustle of paper (from the food he's tucking away in his cupboard) and the bed being made up. Then the figure disappears again, and the only sound is the occasional suspicious noise from the lavatory.

Approximately three o'clock. I have to get up to use the tin under my bed, which, to be on the safe side, has a rubber mat underneath in case of leaks. I always hold my breath while I go, since it clatters into the tin like a brook down a mountainside. The potty is returned to its place, and the figure in the white nightdress (the one that causes Margot to exclaim every evening, 'Oh, that indecent nightie!') climbs back into bed. A certain somebody lies awake for about fifteen minutes, listening to the sounds of the night. In the first place, to hear whether there are any burglars downstairs, and then to the various beds – upstairs, next door and in my room – to tell whether the others are asleep or half awake. This is no fun, especially when it concerns a member of the family named Dr Dussel. First, there's the sound of a fish gasping for air, and this is repeated nine or ten times. Then, the lips are moistened profusely. This is alternated with little smacking sounds, followed by a long period of tossing and turning and rearranging the pillows. After five minutes of perfect quiet, the same sequence repeats itself three more times, after which he's presumably lulled himself back to sleep for a while.

Sometimes the guns go off during the night, between one and four. I'm never aware of it before it happens, but all of a sudden I find myself standing beside my bed, out of sheer habit. Occasionally I'm dreaming so deeply (of irregular French verbs or a quarrel upstairs) that I realize only when my dream is over that the shooting has stopped and that I've remained quietly in my room. But usually I wake up. Then I grab a pillow and a handkerchief, throw on my dressing-gown and slippers and dash next door to Father, just the way Margot described in this birthday poem:

> *When shots ring out in the dark of night,*
> *The door creaks open and into sight*
> *Come a hanky, a pillow, a figure in white . . .*

Once I've reached the big bed, the worst is over, except when the shooting is extra loud.

Six forty-five. Brrring . . . the alarm clock, which raises its shrill voice at any hour of the day or night, whether you want it to or not. Creak . . . wham . . . Mrs van D. turns it off. Screak . . . Mr van D. gets up, puts on the water and races to the bathroom.

Seven-fifteen. The door creaks again. Dussel can go to the bathroom. Alone at last, I remove the black-out screen . . . and a new day begins in the Annexe.

Yours, Anne

POCKET PENGUINS